not

poems

moments

of

Awareness

not

poems

moments

of

Awareness

donna thomson

MERLINWOOD BOOKS • EAST BLOOMFIELD, NY

ISBN 978-0-9913882-6-4 paperback

Cover photograph: Joshua Michael Schrei
Design: www.merlinwood.net
Published by Merlinwood Books

this book is dedicated

to the welfare

of all beings everywhere

not

poems

moments

of

Awareness

foreword

this book is an offering
from myself to myself
and to all beings everywhere
in celebration of Awareness
on the occasion of my 70th birthday
september 7th 2018

my life has been a journey in Awareness
my path
is the path of Awareness

ever since i can remember
i have experienced
moments of heightened Awareness
where everything falls into place
and is illuminated
by the light of Awareness

for seven decades
Awareness has lived
breathed
thought
loved
laughed
wept
in this world
as donna

guided by

an Awareness

beyond my individual awareness

my life has unfolded

its mystery and magic

its joy and sorrow

its inherent purpose

these words

are my offering

from the depths of my heart

the present moment

from dawn

to midnight

midnight to dawn

is radiant with

the light of Awareness

each breath

reveals

what

is

now

days

months

years

go by

time breathes me

into ever greater consciousness

of its passing

dreams recede

into dreams

past and future

day and night

winter

summer

youth

age

time

timeless

the present has no opposite

moments

echoes of eternity

eternally arising

moments

shimmering threads

woven

into

my life's tapestry

⊙

between past and future

there's a breath

that's all

no present moment

one exhalation

the inhalation

is

already a memory

what we call the present

is

simply

Awareness

of

the Awareness

always

present

⊙

deep in the breath

beyond knowing

peace blossoms

oh the days

the translucent shimmering days

past

present

future

blend

in a single stream

time disappears

into itself

it is we who divide

the minutes and the hours

time indivisible

flows relentlessly

exquisitely

beyond itself

into the eternity

known also

as the present moment

⊙

dawn

awake

in the deep night

lost in the breath

enfolded in pure darkness

nestled at the heart

of the great mother Awareness

the sense beyond sense

feels her embrace

the ear beyond the ear

hears her hum

the song of creation

whispers in the breath

always

dawn arrives

a day is born

☉

darkness before dawn

morning meditation

mind spirals inward

to the single point

Awareness

breath

rhythm

inhalation and exhalation

mind spirals outward

disperses

into glittering galaxies of thought

outflowing Awareness

inflowing Awareness

breath

pulse

heartbeat of all that is

exquisite vibration

the peace that arises

as Awareness returns

always

to itself

⊙

should have

could have

would have

(if only i'd known)

might have

all arise

in the early morning darkness

of almost seventy

one breath

two breaths

three breaths

regret

hope and fear

sickness and health

faith and doubt

near and far

success and failure

joy and sorrow

then and now

all spiral

into the dawn

one breath

two breaths

three breaths

the lead

of what might have been

melts

into the gold

of what is

awake in the night

worried for the world

magical alchemy of breath

Awareness expands

holding all

hope and fear

defeat and victory

anger and acceptance

seeing and sorrow

here i am

again

ancient rhythms and tides of samsara

eternal presence of love and Awareness

no way out

only through

the wheel turns

in the dawn light

a bank of dark clouds on the horizon

a single star above

$\odot$

morning

sitting with the breath

becoming the pulse of the universe

Awareness within Awareness

breath beyond breath

beginning this day

with the ineffable dance

of

stillness

⊙

yesterday i was given

the butterfly's teaching

all there is to do

is drown yourself

in the sweetness

of this blossoming world

awake in the night

i dwell awhile

in the heart

of the flower

arising this morning

the news is the same

i am different

⊙

walking out my door

this early morning

i step into the temple

that transcends time

that rises eternally

with every breath

this morning

earth and air and fire and water

dawning light

single star

cold wind

elemental forces

i am woven of these

the weaving is never done

it breathes

a living temple

of cloud and rain

lightning and thunder

mountain and valley

winter and summer

seed and blossom

stone and star

this moment

the soft chill air

of a birthing autumn day

the whisper of winter to come

the wildflower seeds

scattered under a new moon

that will melt deep

into the earth

and dream themselves

into blossoms

the inhalation

the exhalation

it is good

it is true

it is beautiful

⊙

time spirals

weaves itself into itself

skin and blood and bone

remember

when

sea and star

mountain and river

tree and stone

earth and air and fire and water

plant

fish

bird

animal

human

all told their stories freely

and

every story

was heard

a time before

knowledge was forbidden

a time when

all was revealed

a time when

everything knew itself

intimately

blood and skin and bone

we are walking memories

longing to remember

dawn

the lake moves in iridescent waves

to meet the sky

the particular blue mist of morning

hides the mountains

five ducks

exactly five

rise up and beat their wings

a few steps further up

a single white swan sleeps

adrift

spiraled into herself

one raven hovers

just beneath the crescent moon

here

a tree in full green leaf

there

another about to bloom

each day begins with its unique precision

its unrepeatable confluence of circumstance

sun rises

above a bed of tulips

petals

red and orange and yellow

encrusted in ice

frozen

in the exactness

of this early morning

day

touch everything so gently

do not disturb

it is all so fragile

so precious

so irreparable

oh we think we heal

and yes we do

and no

we never heal

everything

is in a constant state of wholeness

at the same time

it is eternally broken

there is the wound

the inexplicable wound

of just being alive

accompanied moment after moment

by the almost unbearable

sweetness

of

just

being

⊙

i walk through love

i walk through sorrow

i walk through joy

through peace and fear

yesterday and tomorrow

i walk in the light

of the rising sun

oh

what torrents of thought

and feeling

make a life

mountain

sky

breath

together

teach me

all i need to know

suddenly i am transfixed

two birds sit in complete stillness

on the tip of an old piñon

down here

the shadow

of myself

seeing

above us

brilliant blue

ripple of white cloud

i walk on

my fingertips touch the air

stroking the skin of the sky

love arises

somewhere

in the distant reaches of my mind

words struggle to surface

to describe

to tell the story

to give it all meaning beyond meaning

oh my mind

moving in waves like the sea

the tides of my mind

ebb and flow

the shadow of myself watches

from a distant shore

the mind subsides

love remains

carries me forward

into this day

words return

here they are

the story

of

my morning walk

oh this world

this self

this morning

sadness blooms in the heart of joy

joy whispers gently in the midst of sorrow

loving Awareness holds them both

in the space

of a single breath

⊙

this morning

driving to albuquerque

i ride the waves of the horizon

mountain meets sky

as sea meets shore

oh this land

bare bones of the earth

naked beauty

uncompromising

this is a place

where one learns to live

on light and air

where one learns to stop

and grow still

in the presence

of a single raindrop

it is enough

to flood the heart

⊙

experimenting

what would life be like

without the word "i"

sleeping

dreaming

waking

thinking

eating

doing

walking

driving

getting out of the car

blinded by light

a red apple shines

from a bare branch

in the morning sun

ah

yes

without that one word

who is blinded

and who shines brightly

⊙

upekkha (pali)

the sublime state of equanimity

my lesson

in equanimity

today

a raven in a dark-clouded sky

above the white mountains

rides the cold winter winds

⊙

winter morning drive into town

snow on the mountains

mist in the valley

icy roads

two ravens circle

sun comes through

no need to elaborate further

this morning rings like a clear bell

in our troubled world

⊙

today

i am drinking

of those waters

that taste of sorrow

flowing from

the deep wells of

human experience

oh buddha

how right you were

greed and anger and ignorance

life is suffering

and yet

and yet

i am drinking also

the waters of gratitude

flowing from

all that holds me here

in this world's embrace

love

a good friend giving birth

bringing new life

yes

my son and his beloved

finding each other

yes

my partner's hand in mine

yes

eternal truths

love that brings Awareness

Awareness that gives rise to love

streams that become rivers

oh love oh Awareness

make me worthy

of these times

⊙

today

all day

the light resembles thunder

dark-clouded

etching the world in gold and silver

a light that pierces

then soothes

demands

then forgives

i move through this light

aware of its breath

seeing

feeling

knowing

the truth of the cosmic body

the universe has its fascia

its organs

nerves

blood and bones

my fingertips brush

the connective tissue

of all that is

this body is a mirror

of the other

it's what i am

a cosmic analogy

my daily prayer

oh thunder beings
you who open the gates of the rain
cloud beings who nourish the rain
spirit of wind that brings the rain
spirit of water that embodies the rain

i recognize your presence
i honor you
i respect your power
i thank you for all you do
to bring the blessing of rain
to this dry land

☉

i've discovered recently

that most of the things

i think i want to say

when allowed enough space

just

disappear

⊙

silence

like color

has

its rainbow hues

silence

like sound

has its rhythms and melodies

silence

like water

is clear

deep or shallow

sometimes muddy

flowing or still

silence

like light

shimmers

radiates

illuminates or blinds

silence

like darkness

can be

fearful or soothing

filled with

beautiful dream

or

terrible nightmare

silence

receives all

gives all

silence

is

a mirror

reflecting

whatever we bring before it

⊙

i notice

the clamor

of the outside world

becomes louder

daily

noise is a way of life

strident voices

fill the emptiness

at the heart

of our nation

i notice

the louder it gets out there

the more quiet

i become

inside myself

space expands

to hold it all

in a single breath

inhalation

exhalation

it's good to live in a place

where

i can see

the stars at night

⊙

yesterday

and the day before

and before

i sat at my desk

and read the news

i could say my heart broke

but i've learned over time

the heart doesn't break

it stretches

wider and deeper and higher

than you think is possible

to hold everything

everything

tonglen

the ancient tibetan practice

breathing in

the suffering of others

holding it in the heart of Awareness

allowing it to transform

breathing it out

as compassion

tenderness

possibility

so i breathe

it's what i know how to do

i lift my eyes

outside my office window

is a deer

golden

in the late afternoon light

so close

watching me

in her gaze

i am held

for a long moment

in the very heart of Awareness

she dips her head

turns

and slowly departs

⊙

today's injury

opens

all the wounds

of all the yesterdays

mysteries of incarnation

dwelling

deep within

reveal themselves

with the gentle touch

of

Awareness

pain opens the inner eye

time and eternity

flow together

in the breath

that union

brings memory

beyond remembering

in the present

this miracle

we call the body

heals

⊙

remember

life whispers in my heart

i exist on the delicate edge

of chaos and order

this word

chaos

from the ancient greek

khaos

the abyss

the vast emptiness

that precedes creation

order

from the latin ordinem

arrangement

pattern

routine

(originally

simply

a row of threads on a loom)

ah

from the abyss

a pattern is woven

we call it life

too much order

we become rigid and dense

too much chaos

we dissolve

in the existential void

for a brief moment

in time

we breathe

we dance

we laugh and cry

we love

on that shifting boundary

the ever receding horizon

the subliminal edge

we call life

☉

oneness

divides itself

into time

the universe

counts itself

into being

dances

to the rhythm of time

and lo

all is born

into infinite beauty

emergence and return

inhalation and exhalation

moments

hours

days

years

time eternally

invites us to

the suffering of its separation

the bliss of its dance

talking with an old man yesterday

(older than me)

mutually regretting

the current state of the world

a moment of timelessness

i think of how many elders

have had just this conversation

since the world began

these days

i begin to appreciate age

the longer view

the deeper acceptance

the wider embrace

the lowered expectation

the heightened blessing

of every day

⊙

the freedom of not knowing

the peace of not judging

the simplicity of allowing

the wisdom of the unnamed moment

seen from above

mountains and valleys appear

as exactly what they are

pure concentration

thrusting itself

into exquisite pattern

waves in a sea of consciousness

crystallized

into time

the plane descends

i am convinced again

the history of humankind

is one long fall from grace

we are exiled from the garden

not by our desire for knowledge

but rather by our ignorance

our failure to recognize

the beauty we come from

the beauty we are

⊙

saints and mystics of every tradition

i have come to tell you something

this i know

from my own loving

my own living

to merge is bliss

union is sublime

but the work of love

the down and dirty

daily

work of love

is to see the other

embrace the other

let the other

be

⊙

oh raven

you who accompany me down this dusty road

the steady beat of your wings

carries my spirit

beyond what appears to be

into what is

☉

I hear the echoes of history

in the strident voices

the culture of insult and scapegoating

the noisy exaltation of ignorance

there is that in me

that is afraid

and there is that in me

that has seen before

the inevitable impermanence

of it all

sometimes i wish to retreat

become a hermit

praying ceaselessly for all of humanity

the good and the evil

the victim and the perpetrator

winner and loser

leader and follower

oppressed and oppressor

destroyer and creator

then a whisper of a voice comes

not strident

gently

piercing

like birdsong in the morning

it reminds me

whether or not lions lie down with lambs

we humans can learn to love one another

indeed

it's our destiny to do so

i am reminded i can do that

now

right where i am

it's such hard work

the activity of love

it requires minute attention

deep desire and intention

profound Awareness

and absolute honesty

with oneself

it takes far vision

to see this possibility

to hear that subliminal whisper

in the midst of all the noise

i'm looking far and high and wide and deep

i'm listening

i'm listening

⊙

this day

it's as though

i'm at the heart of a shell

in the depths of the sea

far away

oh so near

and all around me

grains of sand

are becoming

pearls

did you stop to see

just now

in the stark and tender

mountain light

the shadows of trees

patterns of grace

illuminated

just there

on the wall

before your very eyes

⊙

ah

yes

the mind is assaulted

by powerful forces

beyond its control

the breath is

its greatest guardian

the belly is the home

of that precious protector

the heart

the resting place

for an exhausted mind

⊙

a story arises in my mind

vimalakirti

the sick bodhisattva

visited by manjusri

the wisdom bodhisattva

let's define terms

bodhisattva

one who postpones

her or his or their

ultimate entry

into

nirvana

in order

lifetime after lifetime

to be of service to beings

to all of us

who are turning

turning

on the relentless wheel of existence

to relieve our suffering

to light the way

so in this story

manjusri is sent by the buddha

to inquire of vimalakirti

why are you ill

and vimalakirti replies

i am sick because the world is sick

today i cough myself into and through

morning meditation

breath

awareness

coughing

merge

grief arises

i've been coughing

for almost three weeks

yes

i've been to the doctor

i'm basically ok now

after meditation

i read the morning news

so predictable

the exact trajectory of these events

the turning of the wheel

vimalakirti's words come to mind

perhaps i am sick because the world is sick

or perhaps

the world is sick

because i am

is this one

is this two

the ancient zen questions

ring

in my heart

and fade

into

the simple challenge of today

and every day

who is responsible

for this world's suffering

and how do i address it

now

this minute

in my next breath

thought

and action

the root of the word

compassion

is

to feel with

that i can do

the temptation of privilege

to close the door

as well as the eyes

of the heart

to find peace

in remembering the breath

and forget everything else

to turn away from the suffering of others

that

is not the way

of the bodhisattva

for the moment

these words

are what i have

to offer

⊙

stories

everywhere

stories dwell deep

in neurons

synapses

cells

stories incarnate

over and over

what if

what i call

self

is simply

one scene

in an immense drama

ancestors stream in my blood

whisper their stories

in every breath

all that has been

will be

has never been

will never be

echoes in my ears

my heart

the words i speak

remembering

the naked city

tv show 1963

there are eight million stories

in the naked city

this has been

one of them

remembering

after my parent's divorce

my mother's apartment

i looked out over montreal at night

small town girl in a vast new world

and thought

how many millions

of stories

more than the grains of sands

of all the deserts

or drops of water

in all the oceans

indeed some days i drown in stories

others i drift

stories have saved me

destroyed me

carried me

dropped me down

into the depths of my

no self

stories have loved me

as i have loved them

stories tell themselves

listen to themselves

are born out of themselves

into themselves

in their beauty and their terror

their sorrow and their joy

their wisdom and their ignorance

forever and ever

amen

⊙

forgiveness

what is
is
it's that simple

forgiveness
the all-encompassing
embrace of Awareness

forgiveness
freedom

⊙

raven drifts in a storm-clouded sky

mist drapes the mountain ridge

ancient memories awaken

what is that melody in my heart

just beyond my hearing

breath breaks

on the shores of thought

finally just

the rhythm of an ancient sea

rising

falling

constant surrender to the wave

of what is

this is my practice

my discipline

my delight

my only refuge

☉

a day

a treasure

an abyss

a moment

a breath

a whisper

a single bead

on an endless rosary

a seed

a blossom

beginning

ending

a space between

yesterday

and

tomorrow

⊙

twilight

twilight meditation

breath unites with awareness

not my breath

not yours

it is the pulse

the universal breath

day breaks on the shore of night

moon swallows sun

seeds of light blossom

in radiant darkness

birth and death

hope and fear

past and future

yes

the dance of duality

displays itself exquisitely

accompanied by

the rhythm

of

the breath

☉

twilight

and the light

is a held breath

gold-misted

in its gentle exhalation

stillness absorbs every thought

every hope

fear

gain or loss

the rise

the fall

night and day

the stone buddha

sits

crickets begin their song

oh thunder beings

you who open the gates of the rain

i await your decision

breath merges into silence

the rain comes

happiness arises

so simple

⊙

have you noticed

sun rises

light breathes

sun sets

the dark breathes

what if

all we are

is the breath

of all that is

the breath whispers

attune

harmonize

merge

become

be

the breath

of

the breath

⊙

two ravens

wing their way

across the twilit sky

oh ravens

what currents carry you

what do you see

do you know the beauty

all around you

oh ravens

what would it be like

i wonder

to simply

be

the beauty

⊙

in the moment

between

sunset and moonrise

it is possible to shapeshift

to become the silverblue air

a breath

a shadow moving

through the sweet stillness

through whispers of trees

mountains echo in the silence

beneath a sky so vast

it absorbs

every word

ever spoken

autumn equinox

we dwell on the delicate edge

of light and dark

a moment of perfect balance

before light slips

into dark's dreaming

⊙

spring equinox

twilight and blue mountains

earth and sky unite

light and dark

in perfect balance

chaos of the world

recedes

into one breath

comes to rest

in a single moment

this threshold between day and night

the infinite

the infinitesimal

space

between

inhalation

and

exhalation

meet me there

☉

i meant to sleep early tonight

the hours went by

now i know

i was waiting for the rain

water spirits

will sing me

into the depths

of dream

⊙

i am drenched in light

it is pouring light

i'm soaked through and it won't stop

the same light i saw leave my mother's body

moments before she took her last breath

and i said

i see you

i see you

i am lifted by light

sifted by light

and returned to myself

i am carried by light

fed by light

held by light

tonight

just now

i close my book

turn off the lamp

and yes

the dark itself

is radiant

⊙

i need ancient songs

i call them from my blood

water of life and time and mother

sing to me of love

sing to me of how it is always thus

sing to me of the river

i know so well

she who surges

who floods the land

she who flows endlessly

timelessly

from then to now

sing to me of the sea

the rhythm of the tides

the wave and the shore

sing to me of sweetness

tenderness

the touch of the mother

the caress of the lover

the joy of birth

the sorrow of death

life beyond life

season after season

time beyond time

ravens wheeling in a silver-clouded sky

the dark of the moon

the light of the sun

oh song of this world

forever in my heart

sustain me

carry me

flood me with love

memory

feeling what has been

in what is

empires rise and fall

within my breath

⊙

midnight

full moon

soul and spirit

moon of tides and rhythms

grandmother of my blood

she who directs

the movements of the waters

oh the seas

that rise and fall

with every breath

the waves

sorrow

joy

love

loss

song

silence

birth

death

this exact moon

since the emergence of time

has poured her light

upon the oceans of the earth

i look to her

for constancy

in her waxing and waning

is eternity

☉

i awake in the night

to the sound of rain

and know

this is what draws me back

lifetime after lifetime

it's that simple

rain falls

a rose blooms

a mother's hand

touches her pregnant belly

the moon appears

clouds clear

dawn comes

over and over

the song of existence calls me

the rhythm of the eternal

eternally arising

the blessing of life

⊙

i have come

after all

to love

the turning of the wheel

circles within circles

day turns to night

light to dark

dark to light

the seed of the opposite

blossoms

in each breath

the longest night

is

the most radiant light

⊙

is this music i hear

inside me

or does it come

from distant stars

or is it the wind

the song of the breath

fills the universe

everything dissolves

into the great harmony

and returns

transformed

⊙

people want to follow their hearts

which heart

exactly

is that

i want to follow the great heart

at the root

the core

the center

the one

pulsing

in body and star

night and day

flood and storm and stillness

seed and flower

that never for one moment

ever stops beating

awake

in the deep dark bright night

of the september full moon

between exhalation and inhalation

in a space so completely familiar

so utterly unknown

the heart whispers

dream yourself

out of yourself

i'm dreaming words

no image

radiant dark

streaming a mysterious language

that disappears

upon awaking

mist

in the morning sun

within us

canyons carved by the waters of experience

older than time

deeper than mind

flooded now

gates opened

what i have learned in this life

when the day seems dark

turn within

listen

there is a voice

beyond thought or feeling

fear and hope

in the subliminal spaces of night

spirit speaks

remember

in the ancient rhythms

of life

of time

of spirit

it is arranged so

each night

in the dark

we return home

to receive guidance

for the journey of the day

the bringing of the light

riding the wave of the breath

becoming the breath

it is not mine

or yours or his or hers

or theirs

it belongs to everyone

and to no one

the great mother breath

breathes us into existence

holds us all

in her profound rhythm

all our lives

and then

when it is time

gently

fiercely

lovingly

breathes us back

into herself

☉

thus have i heard

in the ancient teachings

of india

pure illuminated consciousness

is

the divine mother

of all

oh great mother Awareness

you are the rain

falling gently in the night

where there is no rain

the river

that floods

the heart

you are presence

where there is absence

Awareness

where there is ignorance

love

where there is hatred

oh great mother Awareness

you are the breath
the blood
the pulse
of my being

my expansion
my contraction

my living
my dying

you
hold
everything
in your embrace
unconditionally

you
are the tenderness
the caress
the tears
the laughter and the sorrow

you are my sustenance

oh great mother Awareness

you

give birth to me

every moment

of every day

she comes

the great mother Awareness

she comes as night

deepest night clothed in stars

she comes as the dark hour

before the dawn

she comes

as the hand that gently soothes

the womb that nurtures life

the arms that embrace

she comes as sleep and dream

the vision from which world emerges

she says

in the depths of night i give birth to day

in the depths of darkness i give birth to light

in the depths of dream i give birth to you

to the world

to the cosmos

my daughters

join me in my dream

come now

dream with me

together we can dream

a different future for this world

together we can dream

a world of love and peace

we can dream a world where once again

animal

plant

human

sun

moon

star

earth

air

fire

water

and

spirit

dwell in right relationship

to each other

dream with me

my daughters

they say it is impossible

a foolish fantasy

an imagination

do not believe that

i come to tell you
the dream is real
as real as your daytime world
no more
no less
the dream does not have to become a reality
it is a reality

the dream simply
has to move
from one world
to another

you are the gateway
through you
the dream enters this world
the dream i ask you to share
is the dream of all eternity
all time
and all that is beyond time

as you dream
you join your sisters who also dream
together we dream

and because day is night

in another part of the world

someone is always dreaming

somewhere always

there is a woman dreaming

dreaming

dreaming

in the dark

an ancient question

once asked by long-ago sages

arises

breathes itself

into Awareness

what do all dreams have in common

simple answer

there is always a dreamer

and who

who

dreams this dream of a life

this dewdrop dream

trembling at the edge

of the petal

of a rose

that blooms

under the sea

deep in the forest

illuminated by starlight

who dreams it

who dreams it all

to paraphrase nagarjuna

one of those old sages

it is all illusion

it is all real

it is neither real nor an illusion

it is both real and an illusion

oh dreamer of this dream

oh dream of this dreamer

i arise in the night

walk through

the dark and silent house

my foot knows the path

my hand knows the word

my heart knows the dreamer

the dream

writes itself

afterword

the path of Awareness is simple

the breath is its gateway

it is a path of constant return

we wander

the light of Awareness seems to disappear

deep inside

at the heart of everything

it's still there

it emerges

and guides us

back to ourselves

Awareness constantly returns to itself

in a single moment

with a single breath

in one period of meditation

throughout our day

in a lifetime

in many lifetimes

our journey is one of constant return

to the home we have never left

note

zen master ryokan is said to have said
when you know my poems are not poems
then we can begin to discuss poetry

people call what i've written poems
i have read enough truly great poetry
to know
my words are not that

these words are exactly what the title says

moments of Awareness
that make up a life

with love
donna

now

i awake this morning

to the thought

of immigrant children

in camps

now

and

other children

in other camps

long ago

i awake to the thought

of native children

torn from their homes

children of slaves

wrenched

from their mothers arms

i awake to this knowing

daily now

all my life i have been walking

on a fragile

narrow

bridge

of

denial

built upon

the suffering of others

and i ask myself

what next

this i know

what i have called

ordinary life

cannot continue as it has

change must come

in myself

in this world

each day

i will not close my eyes

i will hold the knowledge

of the suffering

of others

close

in my mind

and in my heart

and let that guide me to

the right action

required by these times

⊙

may all beings be

happy

peaceful

and

free of suffering

for more about donna and her work

www.sourcepointtherapy.com

the vibrant life: simple meditations to

use your energy effectively

sentient publications 2006

sourcepoint therapy: exploring the

blueprint of health

merlinwood books 2015

Made in the USA
Middletown, DE
16 October 2021